To Ivy
Thanks for ge
and helping to save 'lives.
Malcolm

Greenbank Primary: First Aid Brought to Life

by

Malcolm Sweetlove

Illustrated by Maggie Kneen

CRANTHORPE
MILLNER
PUBLISHERS

ISBN 978-1-912964-77-2 (Paperback)

www.cranthorpemillner.com

First Published (2021)

Cranthorpe Millner Publishers

This book is dedicated to my beautiful and loving wife, Catherine Sweetlove

Fill the table below in with your details.

It's very important you know your exact home address if you ever need to make an emergency phone call.

Home address: ....

....

Post Code: ....

Home Tel. No. ....

Mobile No. ....

School Address: ....

....

School Tel No: ....

Mum Tel No: ....

Dad Tel No: ....

Guardian/Carer ....

Contents

Foreword

By Professor Lawrence Cotter

Consultant Cardiologist and (Honorary) Professor of Medical Education (Retired) University of Manchester and Manchester Royal Infirmary

Malcolm Sweetlove has written this interactive book on first aid which is both very timely and extremely valuable. It is addressed to young people aged from 9 to 12 but the information it contains will be useful to them throughout their lives. The range of topics are relevant to any age. In the medical profession, all doctors, nurses, dentists have to pass Basic Life Support on a yearly basis and this is covered in **Greenbank Primary: First Aid Brought to Life.** There have been many instances of where a young child has been able to phone emergency services for assistance for a parent who is having a seizure, severe asthma attack and so on.

Malcolm has covered a whole range of incidents where a relatively young, trained attender could make an enormous difference to the outcome. Nearly everyone, from the age of about 7 years old, can be trained to give cardiac resuscitation, which will preserve life until expert medical help arrives. This is a first-class guide, for young people, to first aid and resuscitation which should serve to reduce the severity of these misfortunes.

Malcolm has that most valuable characteristic of all superb teachers: infectious enthusiasm.

I am sure this important contribution will be a great success.

An area where this guide should be particularly useful is in the care of episodes of sudden cardiac arrest. In the UK 170,000 people die of a sudden cardiac arrest. Furthermore 30,000 have a cardiac arrest outside hospital – the vast majority of whom die. **This is a massive public health problem.**

When a person has a cardiac arrest it is often stated that tragically, "They had a massive heart attack and died – nothing could be done". This is misleading and not well understood. A person having a heart attack does not necessarily go on to have a cardiac arrest and, if this book is followed, young people can appreciate that and do something to aid survival in both events.

Often what happens in an emergency, is that no one nearby feels able to help. It is often the case that people have a fear of making mistakes, usually due to a lack of knowledge. **This book begins to tackle this issue.** Children absorb knowledge like sponges and if provided with the proper skills, can go on with no fear of failure.

To quote Lizzie Jones MBE: 'Teach our children, change our future.'

Malcolm has that most valuable characteristic of all superb teachers, infectious enthusiasm and I am sure this important contribution will be a great success.

Fainting

It was June. It was hot and, just like a British summer, humid. There was a distinct lack of air.

Jake, Harry, Ed and Dan were sitting in assembly at school. Jake Matthews was everyone's best friend. He was taller than the rest and a natural leader. Born with an air of authority, all the children looked up to him as Head Boy. He suffered from asthma badly but never let this stop him from doing what he wanted – as long as he was careful.

He was glaring at Harry with twisted eyebrows as shuffling noises had grabbed his attention. Harry was digging his index finger into Dan's side in an attempt to get a reaction. And to be honest, to see if he was even still alive.

"Ouch!" Dan gasped. "Get off! Stop it!"

Harry, whose only real interest in school was playing for the football team, was a good lad, albeit with a short attention span. He played in Goal and all the kids nicknamed him 'The Cat' after the famous footballer with the same nickname. He didn't like being stuck indoors - Harry loved being out in the fresh air and sunshine. It was always dark before he'd return home after being out playing with his friends. And he had a lot of friends – he was the type of kid that would never let you down. He always did his homework (quickly!), he never missed school and if the staff at Greenbank Primary ever wanted a job doing Harry was there to do it properly. He was also as nutty as a fruit cake and as daft as a brush. He was also a bit of a practical joker.

Mr Griffiths' huge, busy eyebrows bore down menacingly on Dan. The headmaster was ready to reprimand him for shouting during assembly; but before he could say a word, Mrs McKenzie, Year 6 teacher, yelped: "Oh no!" and she pointed frantically at Ed.

Ed had turned pale, grey, even a little green. He had collapsed onto his side.

"Ed's fainted!" Jake shouted.

Mr Griffiths moved rapidly through the assembly, scattering some of Year 3 like confetti at a wedding. The room erupted into chatter.

"Quiet everyone, we're trying to get Ed sorted," Mr Griffiths remonstrated with the babbling masses. "Mrs McKenzie, please would you get both of Ed's legs in the air, we need to get some oxygen to his brain. Harry, stop messing with Dan and go and fetch a chair from the classroom!"

Harry and Dan's faces went the colour of a ripe plum and Harry sped off on his mission. He came back seconds later with a chair.

"Good boy, Harry, thank you. Bring it here so we can put Ed's legs on it. Everyone stand back and just give him room to breathe, I'm sure he'll be fine."

"What's up with him?" Harry asked, concern etched on his face for his friend.

"Don't worry, Harry. I imagine it's just the stifling heat in here; there's no fresh air."

"And he said he skipped breakfast today!" Dan chimed in. "That's not good, is it, sir?"

"Spot on, Dan, well done. We must always have a healthy breakfast to start the day."

Ed was coming round now and had a rosy glow to his cheeks. His friends all breathed a sigh of relief.

Activity:

Use the words below in discussion with your group and/or with your teacher to write some sentences about what happened to Ed.

breakfast	circulation
hot	air
humid	legs
oxygen	calm
brain	recovery

Stings

The day got hotter and hotter. All the windows of every classroom were open, it seemed, at Greenbank Primary School. Year 6 were finishing off their project on Sir Winston Churchill. It was going to be home time soon.

Mrs McKenzie was quizzing the class on key events.

"And so, let's see…" she scanned the room for someone to ask and landed on Ali. "What was the first war that Churchill was first involved in?"

"Erm … erm …" Ali's face was screwed up as if he were mimicking a British Bulldog.

Ed had his hand up high and was bouncing up and down off his chair. "Miss! Miss!"

"Ed, what have I told you about that? You look like a Jack-in-the-Box that's had 3000 volts passed through it! Calmly, Ed. calm." The kids in the class laughed good-naturedly.

"The Boer War, miss."

"Well done, Ed, yes. And can you remember what he did in that war?"

"He was a journalist, miss."

"Well done, Ed. Good work."

Harry had his big goalie's hand up.

"Yes Harry?"

"Wasn't Churchill an alcoholic, miss? My mum told me he was. She said he liked a good swill ... I don't know what that is, miss. Is it a type of wine, miss?"

"Well, yes, I suppose he did have a liking for champagne and brandy." Mrs McKenzie was keen to move on.

"Well, how did he still make all those decisions or even walk, miss? He smoked cigars as well didn't he, miss?"

"Yes Harry, let's move on. He still worked tirelessly for the country and virtually everyone smoked in those days. It was just after that that we found out that smoking can cause cancer. Right, moving on..."

It felt like forever that they were being quizzed on Churchill in that suffocating heat but at long last the bell for home time went. The relief of getting out into the fresh air was immense! Their saviour, the ice cream van, was 20 yards down from the school gates. There was quite a queue but Harry was at the front with Dan.

They both ordered the same ("A 99 please with raspberry sauce!") and were pleased with themselves that they had got theirs and were not having to queue in the heat anymore.

A wasp was buzzing around Dan's ice cream. Irritated, Dan swiped at it a few times. In his haste he dropped his ice ream! The ice cream lay in a sad puddle on the floor while Dan was continuing to swipe and swat the wasp, and the wasp was getting increasingly angry. Not only was it being kept from the delicious ice cream, a marvellous meal for a wasp, but it was also not enjoying the attempts to kill it!

"Just stay still and it will go away eventually," Harry advised helpfully. But Dan was too flustered and he continued to swipe wildly at the wasp. Furious now, the wasp stung him! It stung him over and over, four times in total, before Dan managed to get away from it.

He was shouting and screaming and nearly knocked some little kids down … and their mums! Dan was yelping, hollering and crying his eyes out. Poor Dan!

But it's worth noting that, had he listened to Harry and just left the wasp alone, he would have been fine – and so would the wasp! If only he'd listened and been more careful.

Activity:

1. How could Dan have avoided being stung by the wasp?

2. Look up how you would treat a sting from a wasp or a bee.

3. What reactions can people have to stings and how might these be dealt with?

Concussion

Year 5 at Greenbank Primary love PE. None of the other classes are quite as fun! Like Maths, for instance.

Lola Matthews kept getting in a tangle with her algebra equations.

"Why do we have to know whether … why!?"

She was getting fidgety and a bit frustrated and had turned to making those old pictures on her calculator she'd done a thousand times. Jasmine, who was sitting opposite Lola, was poking her tongue out at Lola and rolling her eyes.

They heard the bell for the next lesson and cheered -Yes! It was PE! Lola and her friends Dotti, Jasmine, Ella and Molly went to the changing rooms.

"I've never played hockey. Miss said we're doing it next in PE. My mum used to play for Humphrington," Jasmine said, proudly.

Miss Bentley was splendidly attired in a lurid green striped top and black leggings with a silver strip down the side. She looked like a tube of toothpaste but the girls loved her for it.

Out on the yard, Miss Bentley instructed the girls that on no account must the hockey sticks be raised above shoulder height.

Ella, not known for her listening skills, was messing around and took a huge arc with her stick - clonking Jasmine on the back of her head.

There was no scream, no fuss – Jasmine was knocked out immediately. She lay on the asphalt – her friends were left speechless in shock! Ella was horrified and began to cry.

"Go and get Mr Griffiths!" Miss Bentley shouted to Lola and Molly. The girls sprinted off and brought the headteacher.

Jasmine started to wake up but she looked dreadful. She was shaking, retching, very pale, cold and covered in sweat (which they learned later was a sign of adrenaline). She was even mumbling and jumbling her words. They were all very scared. Miss Bentley called 999.

When someone comes back to consciousness, we should assess how poorly they are. Concussion is very serious. If not monitored properly it can lead to compression – a bleed onto the brain which is life threatening.

- ☐ Look in their eyes. If one pupil is large and one is small that is a head injury. If they are also pale, cold and clammy, they have concussion.

- ☐ You should ask them questions. What's their name? Where do they live? What day is it?

- ☐ If you have a torch, shine it in their eyes. Explain what you are doing first and ask their permission. Both pupils should shrink to a smaller size.

- ☐ If the pupils do not change size in light or they can't answer the questions, phone emergency services on 999 and ask for an ambulance.

Activity:

Here are the RED FLAGS (danger signs) for a bad concussion. Learn them and test one another on them.

RED FLAGS:

- ☐ Neck pain or tenderness;

- ☐ Double vision;

- ☐ Weakness/tingling/burning in arms or legs;

- ☐ Severe or increasing headache;

- ☐ Seizure/convulsion/fit;

- Loss/deterioration of consciousness;

- Vomiting;

- Increasingly restless/agitated/combative.

Making a 999 call

1. Ask for the correct emergency service.

2. Describe properly what is wrong with the casualty:

   a) Are they breathing?

   b) Are they unconscious?

   c) Are they vomiting?

   d) Are they looking a funny colour?

   e) Can they speak?

   f) Are they bleeding?

   You should mention anything at all that you think is important.
   Add some ideas of your own:

   1.

   2.

   3.

3. Say where you are. Make sure you know <u>your</u> home details (refer to the first page! It's very important you know this).

4. Keep your mobile on speaker phone and keep the emergency service people on the line.

   Why should you do this?

5. After you've made the call you should, if possible, try to find a defibrillator.

Activity:

1. When you are making a 999 call why is it important to be very clear when describing what is wrong with the casualty in as much detail as possible?

2. When you are making a 999 call why is it important to make clear what your **exact** address is?

3. An ETA is Estimated Time of Arrival. Why might that be an important piece of information?

4. Write a story involving a 999 call being made.

112:

112 is an alternative number to call. This applies in the UK but also throughout Europe and most other countries in the world. If you do not know where you are you can phone 112. When you have no signal on your phone or you want to make a silent call (if you were under attack or it is too noisy to speak) you can set your smart phone to make a text call to 112. You send a text message with the word 'register' to 112 and when you get a reply you just reply 'yes'. Your phone number is then registered to 112. Text might get through where a phone call may not. It hunts for any mast and has a small piece of information. If there is no network or signal the text will not get through unfortunately but it is always worth trying. If you are using someone else's phone and you do not know the security password you hold the on/off button and the volume button at the same time and it will automatically ring 112.

Panic Attacks

Lola, Ella and Dottie were busy researching the Charge of the Light Brigade; a Year 5 project. They had been working on this particular project for what felt like years now! How had it only been three weeks?

"How could the generals have got the commands so wrong? They sent hundreds to their deaths for no good reason. They made a proper boo boo … like you did getting out of bed this morning, Ella!" Lola laughed.

Miss Bentley glared at Lola. Miss Bentley was usually as cool as a cucumber but today was different. Today OFSTED had descended onto Greenbank Primary with no warning like evil little bats. Even Mr Griffiths was feeling the pressure. Miss Bentley, usually a picture of rosy healthiness, looked pale and worried. Tiny trickles of sweat were starting to appear on her forehead. That had never happened before. Her class had never seen her look so flustered as she begged them, once again, to *behave*!

"Shut it, Lola!" Ella snapped loudly at her friend. "You look like you've been hit by a bus!"

"GIRLS!" shrieked Miss Bentley. They looked up in total shock: Miss Bentley does not shriek … ever. She was going bright red.

Just at this extraordinary moment the classroom door creaked open.

Silence…

Then, more creaking.

Mr Griffiths entered slowly, clearly trying his best to look calm. The children and Miss Bentley knew better though: his eyebrows were knitted together and exaggeratedly high, as if he'd just seen a ghost or a vampire stalking the grounds. Behind him was a suited and booted, bald gentleman with a clipboard so huge it could have been seen from Space.

"Miss Bentley, this is Mr Peabody. He will be with you until break."

Mr Griffiths flashed a smile at Mr Peabody who completely ignored him. Peabody walked quickly to Miss Bentley's desk and sat down with an air of authority given to him at birth. Mr Griffiths backed swiftly out of the room.

The children started talking again after this strange and unwelcome intrusion, not realising in the least how rude they were being.

"Children! Quiet!" Miss Bentley tried to call out in an authoritative tone but her voice cracked and no one listened to her at all. She cast an anxious glance at Mr Peabody who was frowning and writing something down on his huge clipboard.

"Children!" Miss Bentley tried again. "By the time I count to 5 I want complete silence! 1 … 2 …"

Jasmine picked this exact moment to whack Dottie with a ruler!

Miss Bentley stood, frozen to the spot. Horrified. She continued: "…3 … 4 …"

The children realised then that she was visibly turning the colour of a ripe plum and quietened down.

"…5. Good, thank you." Miss Bentley took a deep, shaky breath, but her cheeks remained puce. "James. Have you got Lord Tennyson's poem in front of you?"

"Yes, miss." James was Miss Bentley's pet.

"Read the first stanza out, James, if you be so kind … uh … please. If … if you don't mind." She was visibly shaking now. She looked very uncomfortable.

"What's a stanza, miss?" Darren said, without even bothering to put his hand up. He had just shouted out!

"Manners, Darren. Hands up if you have a question," Miss Bentley said just a bit too loudly. She hadn't meant to shout – it was like she couldn't even control the volume of her voice anymore. "I don't answer questions with no hands up. You know that."

"Who is Tennyson, miss? Is it the Brigade's cat?" Lola asked, her hand waving lazily in the air.

"Miss, can I ask? What's a poem?" Jasmine asked, sniggering.

Miss Bentley flashed a full glare at Peabody who was enthusiastically scribbling on his clipboard.

"Darren. Would you like to answer your question again but with your hand up this time?"

Clearly not. Darren couldn't see the logic of this. It had been and gone. In any case, he was in a sulk. He was avoiding eye contact.

"A stanza is a verse or a paragraph in poetry … if you like." She was struggling.

Peabody was scribbling, audibly, like a demented chimp.

Miss Bentley began to breathe rather loudly and fast. Her face was now the colour of beetroot. She tried to take another deep breath but didn't succeed. She stumbled backwards and leant against the desk; a strangled groan escaped from her pursed lips.

"Are you OK, miss?" Lola kindly enquired.

Miss Bentley could not reply. She was making gasping noises and clutching at her throat.

"Miss isn't well. She's can't breathe!!!" Ella said in a scared voice, getting up to help Miss Bentley.

Peabody's pens flicked out of his fingers and titter-tattered on the wooden floor. Even he was concerned.

Miss Bentley was now making some awful groaning noises. She was struggling to get her breath.

"Girl, go and get the headmaster. Quickly!" Peabody commanded Jasmine. Then he stood there rigid, not having the first clue as what to do next.

Lola said, "Right, I know, this is like my Aunty Sandra. She has panic attacks. Let's get miss out of here and into the staffroom where it's quiet. We can calm her down in there."

The whole of Year 5 rose, as one, to their feet.

"Sit down!" bellowed Peabody, dropping his clipboard with a clatter to the floor.

No one took any notice. Lola, Ella and Dottie had hold of Miss Bentley who was now breathing like a badly tuned car engine. The girls got her through the door and into the staffroom.

Activity:

What was tried in order to help Miss Bentley?	What was the mistake?	What should have been done so that Miss Bentley will fully recover?
Given a cup of tea with two sugars in		
She was laid down on the floor with her feet raised up on a chair		
Placed in the recovery position		
She was reassured that Peabody could watch her lesson after break		

Was surrounded by colleagues and children all wishing her well		

Select which of these sentences best fit into the empty boxes above:

Miss Bentley should be sitting on a chair with someone sitting in front of her encouraging slow, steady breathing.

By putting Miss Bentley on the floor, we are not helping keep her airway open.

Talking calmly to Miss Bentley would be best.

Recovery position is for people who are unconscious but breathing not for people having a panic attack.

Only one person should be talking to Miss Bentley.

When someone is breathing fast in a panic attack giving them food or drink is not a good idea. They could choke.

Miss Bentley should be sat on a chair and someone model the breathing rate 'breathe out for 3 (1-2-3), breathe in for 4 (1-2-3-4), breathe out for 5 (1-2-3-4-5).

The inspector watching the lesson after break is likely to bring on another panic attack.

People gathering around is going to cut down the oxygen levels to Miss Bentley.

Miss Bentley should be left to teach without interruption for the rest of the day.

Discuss what could be causes of panic attacks. List as many as possible in your groups. Then, design a presentation that the whole group is involved in delivering.

Key Points

1. Your presentation must inform and explain what the condition is, why it happens, how can we see it happening and what we can do to get that person better again.

2. Act it out. Have a drama element where the people in your group act out the scene.

3. Have an element of audience participation. Design an activity for your audience that helps their learning. This can be a wordsearch, worksheet, quiz, whatever you like. Try to think of an activity that gets the audience's attention and participation.

Choking

It was another hot June day in Humphrington and Mum Matthews was listening to the radio and finishing off last night's Chinese take away. She had her head in the clouds and felt light and nimble despite consuming a whole field of egg fried rice and chicken in kung-po sauce. Her favourite tune came on the radio and she merrily started bopping away, paying no attention to what she was eating. During one particularly energetic skip, she swallowed a piece of chicken without realising it still had a bone inside! She was swallowing the food far too fast. *Gulp*.

Instantly, she realised that the mouthful was blocking her airway. She vomited half chewed rice across the kitchen floor. She'd made a good job of pebble-dashing the tiles although she wouldn't necessarily have chosen congealed egg splattering to do it with.

She got that feeling. You know: when you've been winded. When some burly kid has banged you in the solar plexus and cut off air. She couldn't breathe!

Dad Matthews was upstairs watching the rugby and someone must have just scored a try because all of a sudden, while she was bent over, choking, little flakes of kitchen ceiling plaster was raining down on her from him stamping his feet with joy directly above.

The sound of Dad Matthews pounding down the stairs reminded one of stampeding steers in a cowboy film. "We won! We-" he bounded joyfully into the kitchen and stopped mid-sentence.

Leaping to action immediately, he bent Mum Matthews over and hit her hard between her shoulder blades with the heel of his right hand 1 - 2 - 3 – 4 - 5 times. Nothing was changing.

He was concerned looking at his wife who was turning a tinge of blue around her lips. Quickly, he put his arms around her tummy from behind. He found her belly button, moved the knuckle of his thumb up a bit and then really jolted her in and then up and out the chicken bone came.

After much coughing, spluttering and vomit they sat holding one another. They both thought that re-decorating the kitchen would be a good idea.

Activity:

1. Discuss what you could try if the person is too big to get your arms around them. Say Dad Matthews wasn't able to get his arms around his wife to do the in and up jolting of his knuckle. What could he try?

2. How would you help a baby when they are choking?

Asthma

July was awakening with a bright, warm sun. It popped up over the yard at Greenbank Primary, throwing a pool of light across the far brick wall like stage lights trying to warm up in a theatre. The wood pigeons were still cooing their rhythmic chanting.

Year 6 were excitedly pouring onto the netball court for their PE lesson. They loved netball but loved Mrs McKenzie more. Jake was excited for the lesson but he had an appointment with the Asthma nurse at Humphrington Hospital and needed to leave halfway through which was a pain.

They had traditional picking of teams by captains and then it was time to get bibbed up.

Within 5 minutes the blue team were 5-3 up. It was an excellent, good-natured game but very competitive. The match see-sawed 5-4; 5-5; 7-5. The blues always kept the edge.

Jake, who was playing for the blue team, had been doing really well - he had netted 4 points! But when Ali went to pass to him, he realised with alarm he wasn't on the court.

A dog had wandered onto the court and was bounding energetically around Jake off to the side. It was Benjie, the Golden Retriever from round the corner. He often wandered into school. It was as if he'd missed out on his education and wanted to return! Benjie was very friendly but the problem was: Jake was allergic to dog hair.

"Miss, Jake's not well!" Ali was shouting at Mrs McKenzie. She didn't hear. The match continued with gusto, enthusiasm, noise and a great deal of bellowing.

Jake was struggling to breathe. He was very pale and covered in sweat. He was shivering and shaking. Wheezing badly.

More people started to notice Jake was in trouble and they stopped playing to rush over to him, Mrs McKenzie included.

"Jake, are you having an asthma attack? You're allergic to dog hair, aren't you?" Mrs McKenzie knew her class well. "Have you got your medication? Have you got your inhaler, Jake?" Jake was struggling to reply. He looked frightened and was really wheezing now. "Ali, go and get Mr Griffiths ... quickly!"

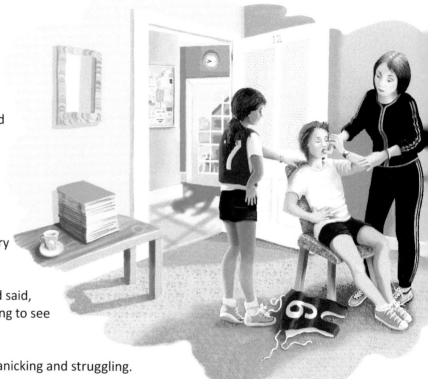

Jake was weakening and looked like he might collapse at any moment. Mrs McKenzie got him away from the dog by scooping Jake in her arms, into the classroom and sitting him on a chair. Harry had found Jake's inhaler.

Mrs McKenzie brought it to take Jake and said, "Take your blue inhaler, Jake. I'm just going to see f you can do it properly."

Normally Jake could, but today he was panicking and struggling. His eyes pleaded with Mrs McKenzie.

"Don't worry, Jake. We'll get this sorted. Try and take deep breaths. Have another go on your inhaler. You're going to be fine." Mrs McKenzie was efficient and purposeful. So kind and reassuring.

But Jake was not fine. He was getting worse.

3 minutes had passed by the time Mr Griffiths arrived.

"Ah, Mr Griffiths," Mrs McKenzie said. "I have this in hand. Could you sit with Jake and see that he uses his inhaler properly. Keep him calm please." She moved away and mouthed to Mr Griffiths so that Jake couldn't see or hear, that 'Jake is really struggling and I'm calling 999'. She emphasised by putting her fingers to her mouth and ears mimicking the phone. Jake should not be disturbed or upset. This would make him worse.

Mrs McKenzie grabbed her phone and dialled 999, telling the operator as soon as they answered, "Ambulance please."

She gave all pertinent details about Jake and what was happening – bad asthma attack, lasting 3 minutes and counting, struggling to take inhaler, can't breathe properly – and then gave the school's full address so the paramedics would have no issues at all finding them.

Once he was in the back of the ambulance, Jake was put on a nebulizer and given medication to stabilize him. One of the paramedics had nothing but praise for Mrs McKenzie's swift and cool-as-a-cucumber actions. She was especially praised for not letting this serious attack to carry on past the 5 minute mark. Jake would make a full recovery as a result. Mum Matthews, Jake's mum, and Mr Griffiths were also really pleased with the way Mrs McKenzie handled the situation. Mr Griffiths said that he would be going to have a word with Mrs Andrews, who owns Benjie, to get her to find a different educational establishment for Benjie to progress in.

Activity:

1. What colour inhaler should be used when a person is having an asthma attack?

2. Write down 3 signs and symptoms of an asthma attack.

    ☐

    ☐

    ☐

3. Why is it important to try and calm a person down who is having a bad asthma attack?

4. Look up what the NHS advice is about how to manage an asthma attack and make a list of key points.

Seizures

Mrs McKenzie loved History and Year 6 were going to love it too, she decided! She also loved Year 6 and this year they were an especially great bunch. They'd do anything for Mrs McKenzie. Even History.

Today, they were going to do a re-enactment of the invasion of Britain by Julius Caesar on August 26th 55 BC. There were to be slave oarsmen and women, merchants, slave traders and legionnaire. The class were watching a documentary about Housesteads Fort on Hadrian's wall. It was really good. They were glued. The programme was showing an assault by Scots and Picts on the Romans' defences which was precisely why the wall was built, to keep out these 'hard-as-nails' tribes. The battle scene went into a slow motion, dream sequence with strobe lighting.

Suddenly, Dan did not look good. He had gone pale. He was cold and clammy. He cried out, went totally rigid and, eventually, fell to the floor. He was thrashing about with his arms and legs that were as stiff as boards. His head was banging up and down on the floor. Blood was coming from his mouth as he was biting his tongue.

Mrs McKenzie acted quickly. She got Ali to go and get Miss Bentley and Mr Griffiths. When Miss Bentley arrived, Mrs McKenzie asked her to take Year 6 and look after them in her classroom as quick as possible. Then Mrs McKenzie moved furniture out of the way and put a cushion from her chair under Dan's head to stop it banging so brutally on the hard floor. Dan was still convulsing but his head was now protected and his limbs were not banging into furniture.

"How long has he been like this, Mrs McKenzie?" Mr Griffiths arrived on the scene, looking flustered.

"About 4 or 5 minutes." Mrs McKenzie was calm and holding herself together.

Dan had clearly wet himself as a large damp patch appeared at the front of his trousers but he had stopped flinching and flailing at least.

"OK. He's stopped. I'm going to put him in the recovery position. That's right isn't it, Mrs McKenzie?"

"Yes, indeed, Mr Griffiths." Mrs McKenzie was relieved that the seizure had subsided.

"Dan. I'm going to put you in the recovery position. Don't worry. Everything is going to be fine."

Activity:

Recovery Position

Before we put anyone in the recovery position, we need to do what's called a Primary Survey.

Remember **DRAB** which stands for:

D = Danger   Check that the area is safe for YOU to continue to work in e.g. are there exposed electric cables that may be a threat to your safety; do people need managing as they are getting over-excited or aggressive?

R= Response   Talk to them and ask them to speak back and open their eyes. Shake their shoulders. If no response, continue with this survey. A response means they are conscious and breathing which is great.

A = Airway   Open the person's airway by placing two fingers under their chin and your other hand on the top of the forehead and tip the head right back. This takes the tongue away from the airway and opens the airway. Keep the head in that position.

B = Breathing   We know that we can assess whether a person is breathing or not by keeping the airway open. Get your head down and look down the chest for 10 seconds. You should see 3 rise and falls of the chest.

Read the table below which explains how to put Dan in the recovery position. Following your reading, illustrate each part in the space given. Make it attractive and colourful.

Illustration	Recovery Position Instructions
	Talk to Dan and use his name – he might still be able to hear everything you are saying despite being unconscious. Before you do any of the steps below, you should tell Dan you are going to do them before you do so he is aware and calm.
	Bend the arm nearest to you at the elbow so it's at right angle to Dan's head.
	Dan is wearing glasses. Carefully remove them and put them in his outstretched hand.
	Check his pockets for any sharp objects so that when you roll him over it doesn't hurt him. Put anything near the hand you'd put the glasses in.

	Take the arm furthest away from you and place it on the side of Dan's cheek (the side nearest to you) and hold it there.
	Take the leg furthest away, bend the knee and put his foot flat on the floor. Hold onto the knee and pull Dan towards you.
	Straighten that leg out so it is at right angles to his body so he won't roll back.
	Move his head gently backwards to fully open his airway

Now that Dan is in the recovery position, he can breathe as his tongue is not covering his airway and if he is sick it will drain away.

Further action can now be taken because you know that Dan is safe. You could phone 999 or 112 and ask for an ambulance: you have an unconscious 11 year old who is breathing but who does need medical assistance

Broken Bones and Grazes

Jake Matthews is a popular lad from Greenbank Primary. He is big for his age, strong, clever, sporty (and good, especially at cricket), likeable, kind, asthmatic and, like most 11 year olds, as bonkers as a banana.

Ali, Harry, Ed and Dan had agreed to meet up with Jake this Saturday to go to the park to have a kick about, get a bus into town, go to the cinema and then have a pizza for tea. Very sophisticated.

"Have you got that world cup ball still Jake? Can we take it with us to the park?" Harry was pleading. Harry was Greenbank's goalie and he dreamed of playing for Humphrington United when he was older. When United's players came to school in PE lessons, he was always keen to impress; to catch their eye as well as the ball - essential work for goalies!

"Yeah, course. Have you brought the Lemonade, Ed?" Jake asked. Ed had a memory like a sieve.

"Oh sorry! I forgot. I'll buy some on the way down."

"Memory like a tea bag, Ed." Ali laughed, punching Ed on the shoulder.

Mum Matthews stood at the door with tea pot arms and a wry smile on her face "Now then. I hope you're all going to be good today. Play nicely. You're being trusted. Right boys?"

"Yes Mrs Matthews," the boys chorused.

"We don't want any complaints from the great and good of Humphrington do we?" Silence. "DO WE!?"

"No," the choir sang.

And with that, off they trooped to the park. Ed slid into the local shop to buy the Lemonade he'd promised. He came out with Lemon sherbets. How can he forget that quickly?! They sent him back in.

In the park, it took ages to spot a good pitch away from tree debris and dog poo. They chose a tree for one goal post and jumpers for the rest. Ali was sorting all this out. He was the organiser. The enforcer. He had it all sorted in no time. In that time the others were passing the ball to one another and having a chat. Trying to decide teams was hard as all of them wanted to be on the same side – Humphrington United! None were interested in the rivals – Knowle City. Harry was adamant that he'd rather have eat frog's tails for tea than play for them. The others giggled at his mixed metaphors.

Dan decided for them in the end. He would be the ref for the first 10 minutes and then they would rotate. Ali and Jake were City while Harry and Ed were United.

"And it's City versus United in this important 6thround cup tie. It's United to kick off."

Harry passed the ball to Ed and immediately sprinted back down field into goal. It's all he knew. He was goalie. The game had to stop while the boys were trying to stop rolling around on the floor, laughing at Harry.

"Harry, you can't just play in goal, you spanner, when there's only two-a-side," Jake laughed.

Off they went again. They followed the ball like a greyhound does a rabbit. They were all going miles off course and towards the road. Dan thought he'd better stop the game when Jake performed a tackle on Harry who went flying into some big branches lying on the grass.

"Arrrggghhh!!!" Harry shouted in pain. He had big grazes on both knees and they were oozing blood. He was writhing on the floor like a premier league footballer when he'd had someone just tap him in the shins. The wounds were quite large and clearly very sore. Harry was usually such a brave soldier but tears were trickling down both cheeks. "Make it stop!" he cried.

From nowhere a very slight, white-haired lady in an overcoat had appeared. Ed had seen her come over from out of her pristine green front door and was at Harry's side. She had seen what had happened. She had a small bowl of warm water, cotton wool, gauze dressing and huge plasters. She was calming Harry down and reassuring him so that he would feel much better any time soon. She cleaned his grazes with the cotton wool dipped in the warm water. There was much flinching and gasping from Harry while the others looked on.

She placed the gauze dressing over the clean, dry wound and applied the giant plasters. Harry was happy and thanked her. She said it was no bother and it happens all the time in the park. Jake had an image of the old lady spending her days gazing out of her front window with the bowl, gauze and plaster ready and waiting at the front door. She told Harry to keep the dressing on until he got home and then soak it off in the bath. It was not to be re-applied.

"You need to get fresh air to it," she said, "so that it will scab over properly."

"You scabby twerp!" Dan jested good-naturedly.

"Hey! Has anyone seen Ali?" Jake asked suddenly, looking around.
A sea of blank faces indicated a 'no'.

"Ali!" The choir sang out loud. "Ali!!" they started shouting
louder when no response came.

"Wait." Jake was pointing with his whole body like a cheetah
stalking a gazelle.

Ali was high up an old oak tree. Stuck. He'd got to that bit in climbing
where to go up would just be plain daft and there didn't seem to be any simple way down. In fact, Ali couldn't see any way down at all.

"What are you doing?" Ed enquired.

"Well, selling second-hand cars to squirrels, obviously! Duh!" Ali was exasperated.

"And now you're stuck, yer Gerbil!" Ed was always helpful in these situations and offered Ali a loud burp from drinking a huge quantity of Lemonade too quickly.

Jake, the sensible one, said, "Can you not get your left foot over to that big branch there and then swing onto that knoll underneath it?"

"Who do you think I am, Tarzan?! No! I can't."

"OK. I'm ringing 999. We need fire fighters." This got Jake funny looks from everybody. They couldn't see any fire!

"Don't be daft. I'll be down in a sec," Ali, the eternal optimist, said.

Jake was already on his mobile.

"Emergency Services, how can I help?" the operator responded. "Where are you? Where is the incident happening, please?"

"Humphrington Park," Jake replied.

"And what is the nature of the incident?"

"My foolish friend, Ali, has got stuck high up a tree."

"What's your name?"

"Jake Matthews."

"OK Jake. Do you require assistance immediately?"

With a loud *CRASH* and a yell Ali came tumbling from the tree and answered the question before Jake could.

"Wow! That was loud ... what's happened?"

"He's fallen out of the tree!! Oh no! Quick ... his ankle looks awful. I can see the bone jutting out at the side!"

"In which case you'll be needing an ambulance now. I'll send one out right now. Are you Lever Road end of the park or Richmond Terrace?"

"We're near Humphrington Road, near to Humphrington station."

"Perfect, stay on the line and I'll talk to you about what you should do. OK?"

"Yes, fine, but I've not much credit left on my phone…"

"Don't worry Jake. This is a 999 call; it isn't using your credit. It's free. Can you go to your friend now please? What's he looking like?"

"A dozy idiot! He's … well, listen for yourself…"

Jake held the phone up so the operator could hear Ali's strangled cries and shouts of pain.

"Did you get that?"

"Yes, thanks for that. Now talk to him and reassure him that the paramedics are on their way."

"OK."

"Now Jake, he'll be going into a bit of shock so keep talking to him, keep him warm. Have you got a jacket?"

"Yes."

"Well put it over him. Have you got anyone else with you?"

"Yes, all my mates."

"Well, can you get a couple to make sure his broken leg does not move? Can you wedge it with some bags?"

"Yeah, Dan and Ed … make sure Ali's bad leg doesn't move."

"Good work, Jake. Now is there someone else who can raise his good leg in the air and hold it there?"

"Harry, you need to hold Ali's good leg up in the air. Ok, that's sorted. Ali's actually looking better. Ed, stop drinking that flaming Lemonade and give some to Ali..."

"Jake, NO! Nothing to eat or drink ... that could make your friend worse and if he has to have an operation it will get delayed. General anaesthetic is 'nil-by-mouth'. Please - nothing to eat or drink. Now, is he looking better?"

"Actually, yes, he is. He's talking instead of screaming now as well. Well done mate ... you're doing fine."

"Brilliant job, Jake. Stick with him.

The siren from the ambulance could be heard coming closer. Ali was going to be fine.

Activity:

Use the descriptions below this box and write them against the correct type of fracture:

Type of Fracture	Description
Closed	
Complicated	
Open	
Green stick	

In this fracture there are trapped nerves and blood vessels.

Common in children. The bone is split and not totally severed.

The skin has been broken by the bone and there is high risk of infection.

A clean break or crack in the bone.

Signs and symptoms

Can you think of any signs or symptoms that would be obvious to your sight, feeling and/or hearing. I will give you one: irregularity where you get lumps and bumps under the skin. Now think of 3 more:

1. _____

2. _____

3. _____

Treatment

Describe below how you could stop the limb from moving:

Nosebleeds

The late afternoon sun dappled through the venetian blinds in the Year 5 classroom and threw itself across the teacher's desk. It was Wednesday and they were studying history: The Crimean War.

Dottie was standing at the front of the class giving a PowerPoint presentation on Florence Nightingale. She had become somewhat of an expert on one of the very first nurses so much, in fact by now, it bordered on obsession.

Her enthusiasm was evident. The conditions described were horrendous in the extreme.

"And so, even though the wounds were clearly fatal on a huge number of British soldiers she never stopped caring for them … their injuries were abysmal to see…" she clicked the mouse and her PowerPoint showed a picture of a pustulous, bleeding leg.

"Urrgggghhhh … Disgusting!" half the wimpy boys were shouting.

"And some injuries were unfathomable in their cruelty…" Dottie put a slide up of a man who had a cannon shot through his leg and a horse who had been spiked by a lance.

"Urrggggghhhhh … gross … stop it!"

Dottie's eyes were wide with excitement as she continued clicking through her slides. "And here you can see Florence nursing a man who had a shell take half his face away. This was her only equipment - a flannel, carbolic soap and a small amount of brackish water, a lantern to see by and the dead and the dying all around her…"

All of a sudden Dottie's nose burst forth with blood. It was dripping down her nostrils at speed and in some considerable quantity. It was splashing onto the remote control for the data projector. It was as if she was there, in battles, and now needed Florence Nightingale! The bright red fluid was getting all over her notes and gadgets in a sticky, red, gooey mess.

Miss Bentley, of course a modern-day Nightingale, launched herself into action.

"Don't worry, Dottie my dear. We'll get this sorted out." She was calm and serene. Not one hair out of place on her well-groomed head. "Sit here, darling, pinch the soft part of your nose and lean forward with your head … that's it … it will stop in no time at all. Ella, go and get some paper towels and soak them in water so we can start mopping. Jasmine, go with Ella and bring some dry towels. Dottie, do not blow your nose. It will make it much worse." If only Miss Bentley had been in charge of the Light Brigade. There wouldn't have been communication issues then.

Dottie looked mortified. She'd been talking so confidently about soldier's legs being blasted off or torsos skewered by lances and here she was now, devastated by a simple nosebleed.

"Keep pinching your nose, darling, and lean a little more forward," 'Florence' Bentley commanded assertively. "You need to pinch for up to 10 minutes and then stop pinching for a full minute."

"Why?" Ella asked.

"Well, to let the blood vessels refill properly so they don't get damaged. And to see if clotting is occurring naturally. Does that answer your question, Ella?" Miss Bentley was fond of using questions to answer questions.

"Thanks miss." Ella smiled.

"For children under 12 years of age, like you, we apply pressure 3 times, 10 minutes each time, with a minute of no pressure in-between. If the bleeding hasn't stopped after that, we should definitely consider ringing 999. But I don't think we'll get to that situation today, dear." 'Florence' smiled at her patient and Dottie instantly felt better.

Mopping operations were fully underway as the bell went for break. Miss Bentley sent the class out into the yard. She put some gloves on and disposed of the sodden towels in a plastic bag and then put that bag in two other sealed plastic bags. She got the caretaker to take them for incineration.

"Now, Dottie, let's have a look … ah yes, it's stopped … definitely. That's good isn't it?"

"Yes, miss." Dottie was still holding her nose. She sounded like she was submerged under water.

"You can let go of your nose now, dear. Have you had a nosebleed before?"

"Actually, I have. I had three at home last week."

"Well, just keep an eye on things and mention it to your mum tonight when you get home. You might need to go to the doctors. But you're absolutely fine now so go and get some fresh air."

"Thanks, miss."

"Dottie. Your presentation was brilliant … brilliant and very bloody … perfect for the Crimea."

Activity:

Fill in the missing words using the cut out words in the box below:

A nosebleed can happen after a _____ to the nose or through high blood _____ or blood vessel damage in the nose. The treatment is to _____ along the front of the nose below the bridge. The person should lean _____ so that their elbows are resting on their_____. Frequent checks every few minutes would reveal if the _____ has stopped or not. If it has not stopped re-apply for up to _____ minutes. At 10 minutes the pressure of pinching should be _____ for a full minute. If after that minute the bleeding has not stopped you should _____ pressure. For a child under the age of_____, if you have been through 3 lots of 10 minutes with a minute of pressure _____ in between and the bleeding has not stopped, someone needs to phone_____. For anyone over 12 years old consider extending for another 10 minutes. If bleeding is not _____ through pressure then you have to consider that there is something more complicated going on.

10   removed   knees   bang

pressure   reapply   stopping

12   released   pinch   999   forward   bleeding

42

Sprains

Year 6 were having a mock spelling and grammar test and you could have heard a pin drop. It was a particularly difficult test, even the teachers thought so.

"Pens down everyone." Blessed relief as Mrs McKenzie called time and collected the papers and praised Year 6 for their dedication and manners. The bell sounded and the boys cheered – school was out at last which meant it was time for football!

They were playing St. Martins, a rival school today, and they all badly wanted to win.

"Don't forget, Ed," Ali was saying, "you're on Tommy Smith. Tommy's a great player and he doesn't like you."

"Thanks Ali, that makes me feel a lot better." Ed was doing some stretching exercises. He'd seen his mum do them before she went for a run. It looked cool so he thought he'd do some. He had no idea why. "Don't worry, Ali, we've got 'The Cat' in goal, ain't that right, Harry?"

"That's me, The Cat, agile and I always land on me feet!" Harry laughed. "Don't you worry lads, nothing's getting past me!"

"I know you're worried, Ali, because it's your first proper game back since breaking your ankle," Jake said, putting a comforting hand on his friend's shoulder. "But you don't need to worry, mate. You're fully healed and look what you've been like in training. David Beckham's got nothing on you."

Jake, the Captain, was good at rallying the troops. Captain Jake.

The whistle blew. Dan couldn't believe the first pass he made. It sailed gently through the air straight on Jake's head and straight into the goal! It was the quickest goal in Greenbank's history. Of course, the whole team were hugging and kissing one another, emulating their heroes they had seen on *Match of the Day*.

"Get up, you dingbats, and back into position." Mr Griffiths – who also desperately wanted to win - had no time for this sort of caper.

The game ebbed and flowed after that for a good ten minutes until Tommy Smith got the ball on the left, cut inside and walloped the ball with his killer right foot. If Harry hadn't have leapt like a puma and got his finger-tips to it, the ball would have broken the net. He really was The Cat! The whole team cheered him. He looked quite pleased with himself. Like the cat that got the cream.

The resulting corner was cleared and Ed picked the ball on the half way line. There was no one near him. He went to pass it to Captain Jake when his left foot disappeared. Oh no! there was a small crater in the ground that Ed hadn't seen and now his left ankle was badly twisted sideways in it.

"Arghhhh! I can't move it. I think it's broken. Arghhhh! Ed was not best pleased.

Mr Griffith's stopped the game and was attending to Ed. "I think we need this looking at in hospital. You live near the school, don't you?"

"yes … Arrrggggghhh! Sir! My mum's at home at the moment!"

"Jake… Go and bring Ed's mum. Ok? And be careful crossing the road!"

Jake sped off without another word.

Back to Ed. "The best thing, Ed, is not to move you. Lay down. And can someone bring me some coats to put on him?!"

Mr Griffiths had obviously learnt a great deal from the Year 5 project on the Crimean War. He was just like Florence Nightingale, mopping Ed's brow, saying soothing things, keeping him warm. He even put a couple of sports bags either side of his injured ankle to stop it moving. He employed Harry 'The Cat' to hold his good leg slightly up in the air. It turned out that this treatment plan was unnecessary as in hospital, Ed had an X-ray which showed that he had a badly sprained ankle and was advised to follow the procedure, RICE.

Activity:

Do you know what RICE stands for?

Why don't you look it up and write an explanation below:

R =

I =

C =

E=

Burns

The grey sky had an extra tinge of grey in it today. It bordered on black. It was determined to set itself as a shield that blocks the sun and was sending arrows of rain to fight it off.

Lola and Jasmine were shivering and skipping around in the yard at Greenbank Primary. It was very cold. Ella, Dottie and Molly sprinted into the yard to join them, wheeling and screaming at the arrows of rain. They were extra noisy and giddy today. This morning Year 5 were going to Humphrington High. They had been going on a cookery course every Thursday morning for the past 3 weeks. Today was their last time.

"Hi you three giddy kippers. You sound like seagulls who are after a pensioner's fish and chips on the prom!" Lola laughed.

Jasmine still had the painful memory of being clonked on the head by the hockey stick in PE. She was smiling warmly at her friends. A smile was just about the only warm thing today. The three amigos made more screeching and cawing noises playing up to their new status of scavenging seabirds.

"Hey Lola. What have you brought for today?" Dottie was really excited for their cookery lesson.

Lola opened her holdall. There was a gleaming stainless steel pan with a glass lid, an onion, olive oil, garlic, minced beef, bacon, Italian herbs and passata. They were making a bolognaise sauce.

"I've got this lot. It weighs a ton. My dad cleaned that pan for about 3 hours last night. You could use it as a mirror!"

"I was a bit last minute. I've forgotten herbs. You wouldn't lend us some would you, Lola?" Ella, besides being Miss Bentley's pet, was a very sweet, loveable girl with no organisational skills whatsoever. "I grabbed this on the way out." Ella was holding up a pan that had seen better days.

"Of course you can have some herbs, Ella. I've got loads. Where's your tomatoes?"

"Oh no ... forgot them as well."

"Never mind. They have some stock in the store cupboard at Humphrington. You can blag some there." Lola, ever the optimist.

"Oh yeah. Good one, I'll put on my best innocent look." Ella was fluttering her eyes and tossing her bunches.

"That pan you've got, Ella. It's ... interesting!" Molly teased.

"Oh yes, this has seen good service."

"And better days," Molly giggled.

"It was my great, great, great grandmother's," Ella explained.

"Was it used in the Crimean War do you think?" Molly was into her stride now.

"It looks more like something Hitler would wear on his head!" Jasmine gave out a huge hoot and everyone collapsed in laughter.

Year 5 loved Thursdays and the trip to Humphrington High. The cookery teacher was a lovely lady whom everyone adored.

They entered the food lab in silence to be greeted enthusiastically by Miss Armstrong, the Humphrington High Food teacher. Then it was straight down to business. Lola, Dottie, Ella, Jasmine and Molly were all stationed along a long bench with built in ovens and hobs. There were knife blocks and chopping boards for each of them. Within minutes, the sound of slicing and chopping filled the air. The recipe was up in lights on the electronic whiteboard and Ella had blagged a packet of passata and some herbs from Miss Armstrong.

All was well with the world and the smell of oil, garlic, onion and herbs were building. It was a mass effort to produce a Bolognese fit for Italy.

Ella was concentrating hard. She was coping ok even with her pot which had a weird way of spinning on the hob uncontrollably like an ice-skating novice. She'd got everything done and the pot was bubbling gently as if relieved that it had made it home from battle. Then into the oven it went at 180°c for 20 minutes.

As the pots were in the oven there was a demonstration at the front by Miss Armstrong on how to make pasta from scratch.

Once the demonstration was finished, they returned to their pots. Ella was not thinking and she reached inside the oven and pulled it by the handles with just her bare hands! The pain was immediate and intense. Her fingers felt like they were fused to the handles. It was agony!

"Arghhhh!!" Ella screamed. Everyone stopped, shocked. Miss Bentley got a bowl of water and threw it on Ella's hands. Ella let go of the pot, crying out with pain, but it hit her bare leg on the way down and burned her even worse. It was the most serious burn Humphrington High had ever seen.

Miss Bentley acted swiftly and took control of the situation.

"Dottie, fill that jug with cold water please and bring it to me, if you don't mind."

"You'll be OK, Ella, we just need to cool your hands down with water. Miss Armstrong," she located the other teacher and beckoned her over, then whispered at her, "please can you call 999."

Neither of them wanted to make Ella scared, so Miss Armstrong left the room to make the call.

"Now, Ella, I am just going to keep cooling your burns with this cold water. Dottie, get another jug and fill it and bring it please. Everyone else, please can you go and sit down."

Miss Armstrong returned. "Right Miss Bentley I have done that. That looks like a 3% burn to me."

Miss Bentley asked, "How do you know?"

"Ella's hand is 1% of the surface area of her body and I think the burn is 3 hands wide. How is the pain now, Ella?"

"It's better thanks, miss."

"Oh, that's good. Miss Bentley, if you and Dottie can carry on cooling for another 7 minutes, please. After 10 minutes you need to stop for a full minute. We can re-apply water after that for another 10 minutes if we need to - I will go and get the cling film. Remember to just place it on lengthways rather than wrapping – wrapping will cook the skin!" Miss Armstrong had learned a lot at a recent Sweetlove Training First Aid Course last month and was proud to be able to show off her new knowledge!

"Thank you, Miss Armstrong. I'm sorry Ella, love, don't worry. Everything will be fine."

Activity:

Go through the sentences below and mark if they are True (T) or False (F).

You could discuss them in your group and with your teacher:

<u>Sentence</u>

You can cool a burn with cold running water.
You can cool a burn by taking the person out into the cold air.
You can cool a burn by putting the limb in a bucket of water.
You can cool a burn with cold running water for 10 minute intervals with 2 minutes in between.
You can use a special gel pack burn dressing if available.
Ella has 7% burns. She should go to hospital.
For such a serious burn it is important to phone 999 or 112 immediately.
You can pop the blisters that form on Ella's burns.
You can cover the burn, once cool, with dressings from the first aid kit that we use for bleeding.
You can cover the burn, once cool, with clingfilm.
You can treat Ella for shock.
You can cool Ella's burns, lie her on the floor and raise her legs.
You can remove clothing from the burnt area.
You can remove jewellery near the burnt area.

Wounds and Bleeding

The sun blazed across the lawn and flower beds of 32 Richmond Terrace and enveloped the well-kept garden like a blanket. The red roses were reaching up in worship of their sun god. The morning dew had evaporated and the newly mown lawn looked like a green carpet. It wouldn't have looked out of place at Wimbledon. Dad Matthews had used his beloved rotary mower to give the lawn stripes after cutting it yesterday evening. Now he was standing in the kitchen admiring his own work with pride.

Today, he was going to play golf with his mates at Humphrington Golf Club, and before he left he had promised Mum Matthews that he would prepare lunch so he set to work.

The salad was chopped and in the bowl with a squeeze of lemon to keep it curling up at the edges and then he started on the main meal. He picked up a large steak knife and set to work, cutting the steak into chunks ready for the sauce.

Suddenly, out of nowhere, Lola and Jake tumbled down the stairs, screaming at each other. They were good children but they were still brother and sister and sometimes they argued – badly!

While they were screaming at each other, they burst into the kitchen, desperate to get their dad on side first...

"DAD!!!" they both shouted at the top of their lungs, making their poor dad jump right out of his skin!

"Arrrrgggggghhhhhh!!!!" he shouted. The knife slipped in his greasy fingers and the sharp blade sliced through the palm of his hand. Blood was dripping fast in big, bloody blobs onto the ceramic tiled floor where it lay like a pool of jelly.

At that moment, Mum Matthews came home and walked into the kitchen, only to be met by total chaos.

"Arrrrggggghhhh!!!" Dad Matthews cried out again. "Darling … help! Help me! Arrrrggghhh!!!"

"It's ok!" Mum Matthews said, rushing to his side. "Kids – get out, will you? There's a lot of blood and you could slip – stay out of the room while I help your dad."

She gingerly helped Dad Matthews over to a chair, carefully stepping over the blood, and got him to place his other hand over the wound and squeeze tightly, compressing it and staunching the blood. Then she found their first aid kit and dressed the wound tightly, binding both ends of the dressing to keep out infection.

Activity:

Fill in the missing words below. Use the words given in the box below to help Dad Matthews:

Get him to place his other _____ over his wound and sit him down on a chair. Talk to him and _____ him that everything will be fine. Get him to _____ his injured hand above his _____. This will slow down _____ and slow the _____. If you have a _____, take out the dressing. Take it out of its plastic wrapper but do not unroll it yet. First, place it length of the cut. This will create _____ and help to plug the wound. Get another dressing and wrap around the plugged wound. Cover both ends of the dressing to keep out _____.

Depending on his general _____ you may need to _____ him on the floor, put his _____ in the air, cover him with a _____ and call _____.

What if you do not have dressing? Improvise. Use scarves, tee-shirts or _____.

Hand   raise   999 or 112   bleeding

responsiveness   tea-towels   infection

reassure   lie   heart   lie   coat or blanket

legs   circulation   first aid kit

Anaphylaxis

Today was a special day for Greenbank Primary School and for Year 5, in particular. It was the annual school trip. Despite having to fill in hundreds of health and safety forms, they had to be so careful these days what with accidents and allergies – none of the kids were allowed peanuts, for instance, because Lola was allergic to them which was very serious indeed - Mr Griffiths was always of the firm belief that the children at Greenbank Primary deserved a fun day out as a reward for all their hard work through the year. Of course, those who haven't worked hard don't deserve to go but this has not happened yet at Greenbank! And because the point of the trip was for the kids to have fun, the teachers didn't even try to pretend there was anything educational involved. Imagine filling a worksheet in whilst you're on the *Flying Whizzer*! No, Mr Griffiths was not going to make Year 5 do worksheets whilst on the rides at Cool Park.

It is a special, and therefore very early, day. They had to be at school for 7:30 a.m. and the coach would be leaving at 7.45 a.m. on the dot! Lola, Molly, Dottie, Jasmine and Ella all stood together in their smart/casual jeans and t-shirts and carrying their bags containing pop, sarnies, a raincoat and a small shop-full of sweets. This was going to be a proper British day out with rain, singing on the coach and kids being sick from overloading on the Haribo.

"I'm going to sprint to *Twisted Tornado*," Molly said excitedly. "Stick with me. We'll run and get ahead of the queue."

"I'm going on *Rocket Launcher* after that," Lola piped up. "My cousin Tommy went on it last week. He says it's sick."

"I hope not. I've got tuna butties for my lunch and I don't want them coming back up all over people's heads!

Ha! Ha!" Dottie chimed in.

"Not that type of sick, Dot! I mean the ride's really good," Lola cleared the point up, laughing.

They fell into a companionable silence, a couple of them munching early on their lunches (they'd be hungry alter!) for the rest of the journey.

Then Miss Bentley got up at the front of the bus. "Come on, girls!" she said. "We'll soon be there, get your stuff ready."

Miss Bentley was resplendent that day in a bright yellow t-shirt and navy blue trousers. She looked dazzling as the sun caught her sunglasses that were clinging to the top of her head. Her hair, as always, was immaculate and swept back under an Alice band. She walked down the bus to check everyone was doing ok – it had been a long journey! – and as she reached Lola, her eagle eyes spotted that a boy opposite Lola's seat was busy trying to open a bag of peanuts.

Quick as a flash, she snatched them away from him. "You know peanuts are banned, Johnny Baker! And look, you're sitting right next to Lola. What were you thinking?"

To his credit, Johnny looked ashamed and apologised to Lola, saying he'd forgotten. But he really should have been more careful.

Not long after, the coach parked up at Cool Park and her charges piled off the bus, greeting her cheerily as they went. She felt on top of the world and glad that the responsibility for the day would be shared between Mr Griffiths and herself. Dottie and Molly's mums had also volunteered to help and were already strategically placed half-way up the coach armed to the teeth with bin bags, sick bags, bleach spray and lots of mopping cloths. They were ready for action. They knew what was ahead. The boys and some girls will already have eaten their lunch, drank most of their pop and consumed a large number of sweets. It could be messy as the coach rounded the series of bends on the winding roads leading them to the motorway on the way home.

Mr Griffiths and Miss Bentley saw all their charges safely off the coach. They knew the kids could be trusted so they told them all, 'Off you go and have a great day – there'll be trouble if you don't!'

Then the adults all made their way to the café for a cup of tea or coffee and a well-deserved slice of cake.

They all sauntered off towards the café without the slightest thought of rides. They were perfectly content and spent their time chit-chatting about the state of the nation, the Cool Park prices, the Humphrington United football team (equally disastrous) and the state of the pound.

Lola, Dottie, Molly, Ella and Jasmine came into the coffee shop looking for the adults. They all looked quite shaken.

"Hi girls. Everything OK?" Mr Griffiths enquired.

"Sir, Ella's had her bag stolen," Lola said.

"Oh no, how did it happen? Did anyone see someone steal it?"

"Yes, sir," Lola coughed. Her throat was feeling itchy for some reason. "This lad from another school just snatched it and then ran off … him and his mates. They were horrible …" she cleared her scratchy throat again. "They were all laughing."

"Ok, Lola, thanks. Are you feeling ok, you look a little red?"

Lola nodded but, in truth, she was starting to feel very hot and light-headed as well as itchy. She shrugged it off and turned away.

Mr Griffiths turned to Ella. "Ella, are you OK? What colour was this bag? Was it that pink handbag I saw this morning? Come here and tell me all about it." Mr Griffiths was a strong leader but first he was a people person.

Ella tried to smile. Tears had stained her face which had gone blotchy. "Well it had £20 in my purse and my coat that Mum had bought me last week. My mum'll go mad. It was really expensive."

Mr Griffiths had warned them all in assembly about NOT bringing expensive items on this trip but he knew it wasn't the right time to broach it now. He'd do it next week in a quiet moment.

"Don't you worry, Ella. I'm sure we can sort something out. We might even be able to apprehend these idiots who stole your bag. Let's try and get a very accurate picture of what has gone missing and, more importantly, what these thugs look like. I can then contact the -"

But Mr Griffiths was cut off when Miss Bentley suddenly shouted, "Lola!" and rushed over to the girl who now looked very unwell indeed. She was very pale and sweaty. Her lips were swollen and red and she was clearly struggling to breathe. Her face was lumpy and she had a pimply rash down her neck. She couldn't seem to stop itching her skin. It looked like she was going to pass out.

"Mr Griffiths! Help me with Lola, she's going into shock. It's her Anaphylaxis, I'm sure of it."

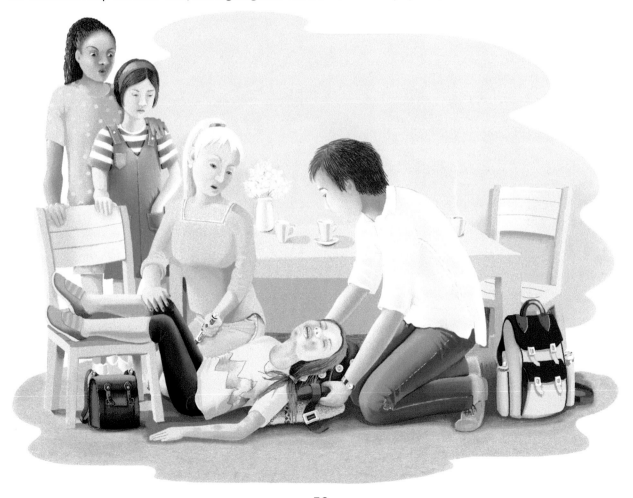

Miss Bentley looked around the small café. A couple on a table not far from them were sharing a packet of peanuts.

She pointed at the unsuspecting couple angrily. "Please could you two move! Now! Get completely out of the café! Take those peanuts with you!"

Mr Griffiths saw their shocked and indignant expressions and tried to placate them. "This girl is allergic to peanuts … it's a severe allergic reaction. It's not your fault but get those peanuts out of here immediately!"

The couple scurried away as quick as they could.

"Mr Griffiths, quick, let's lay her on the floor and get her legs across this chair …"

The staff and customers were all gathering to rubber neck so Miss Bentley turned to Dottie's mum and asked her to keep everyone back. "And can you phone 999 and tell them that we have a 9-year-old girl who is going into Anaphylactic shock, tell them exactly where we are, tell me when you've made that call."

"Sir," Ella was pulling at Mr Griffiths' shirt. "She's got an EpiPen in her bag. Here, look." Ella got it out of Lola's cloth, summery bag.

"Give it to me, Ella. Quickly, love." Miss Bentley held out her shaky hand. Ella passed her the pen. Miss Bentley removed the blue top and plunged the orange end into the top of Lola's thigh. It made a big 'click' noise as the needle shot into Lola's muscle. Within seconds Lola was coping a little better with breathing and had more consciousness.

"The ambulance is on its way. It will be 10-15 minutes," Dottie's mum said when she returned.

"I've always wondered what that pen of hers does," Molly said in an awed voice as she watched the ever-in-charge Miss Bentley work.

"The pen releases adrenaline into the bloodstream and shuts down leaking cells, Molly," Miss Bentley said. "In Anaphylactic shock, cells leak because too much histamine is pouring out of the immune system caused by the thing the person is allergic to. With Lola, it's peanuts. The adrenaline shuts those cells down again and tightens them up in seconds."

"Right." Molly was trying to take all this in. It had been quite an eventful trip so far. "Is she going to be OK?"

"Oh yes, you know our Lola's a fighter. We'll need to get her in hospital to be checked over though. Mr Griffiths, I've got the other two pens for Lola here. In my handbag."

"OK. Good. How long ago did I inject that last one? Oh no, I didn't look at my watch!"

"I did." It was Ella. "It was 3 minutes ago, sir."

"In which case, get the next pen ready. I'll tell you when 5 minutes has gone past and then you inject the next one. Remember, after injecting for 10 seconds take the pen and needle out and gently rub her thigh. It will help distribute the adrenaline."

"Yes, thanks."

The other girls looked on anxiously. This was the first time they had seen Lola have an attack. It was frightening. The good thing was that her breathing was better. Her face was swollen up and she kept really itching her scalp and tummy.

"OK, Miss Bentley, 5 minutes is up."

Click. The second auto-injector EpiPen went in.

"Why's it called an EpiPen?" Molly asked. "She's not epileptic, is she?"

"No, Molly. Epi is short for epinephrine – the international name for adrenaline."

"Oh, I see. Thanks."

The second dose was now really improving Lola. Her breathing was nearly back to normal and the crowd could hear the sirens of the ambulance.

Lola made a full recovery. Ella got her bag and its contents back.

All's well that ends well.

Activity:

Research the answers to these questions

1. What can a person be allergic to?

2. What are the main signs and symptoms of anaphylactic shock?

3. What are the main things you could do to help them?

4. How many people in the UK suffer from anaphylaxis today?

5. Try and find out about a case of anaphylactic shock that got in the news. What happened?

6. Which organisations help people understand anaphylaxis?

CPR

It was a grey day in Humphrington. The day had begun with some light drizzle and a cloudy sky. Now it was just grey and some darker patches were threatening to deluge the good earth with water on biblical proportions.

It was a typical school day start for the Matthews family. Dad had left for work already. Not that there were any visible signs of his existence in the kitchen. No mug, no bowl, no cutlery. All washed, dried and put away.

Mum Matthews was getting juice and coffee sorted out and getting the breakfast cereal out. She was on toast alert should Jake have one of his faddy fits. 'I hate cereal!' That type of thing. She wasn't in the mood for it, not today! She had promised her mum, the kids' grandma, that she'd take her to the train station that morning so she could go and visit her sister by the coast. It would be good for her to get some sea air and she was very much looking forward to the trip, but she was a very fussy and picky old lady and Mum Matthews, no matter how old she was, still desperately sought her mother's approval. So, she couldn't be late!

She packed the kids off to school after relatively little cajoling and had time for a very quick sigh of relief before she jumped in the car to brave the traffic on the way to her mother's.

The traffic was worse than usual (just her luck!) and she sat through several banks of lights in several banks of queues. 'Why is nothing simple and straightforward?' she thought to herself. On the bright side she had enough time to write out her shopping list and the radio was a pleasant distraction.

At long last she got to her mum's house and knocked at the door.

"Hi Mum," she said when her mum answered the door. "Sorry I'm late ... the traffic was dreadful."

"Yes dear no worries. Only problem is I can't find my shoes."

"They're on your feet, Mum."

Looking down. "So they are. Well there's a thing."

"How are you feeling, Mum?" Mum Matthews said when they were on their way to the station (not nearly as much traffic in this direction, thank goodness!) "Excited to be seeing your sister and to be getting some sea air?"

"Yes dear, it will be grand. We've always got on well. I won't out stay my welcome mind. I'll be back a week on Wednesday. That's long enough."

"That's great, Mum. You'll have a lovely time. Did you see Dr. Springer about your blood pressure tablets?"

"Oh yes, dear. They were making me feel so ill. He's put me on a different one and it's a lot better. Yes. Good. Thanks love. Mind you it's difficult taking all my pills these days. There's 10 tablets a day for this that and the other. It's a right to-do. It's nearly morning coffee time by the time I've got them all down. It's like having a job! Ha!"

"Never mind, Mum. At least you got sorted out before your trip so you can properly enjoy yourself. How are you feeling today?"

"Well, do you know ... I don't know if it's your driving or what but I feel a bit sick. Plus I can feel a bit of pins and needles in my left arm. It'll go off, no doubt."

Mum Matthews didn't like the sound of that. "When did this start, Mum? And don't say as soon as I picked you up because I'll take you straight back home again!" Funny how roles reverse with age.

"It was, I suppose, when I got up in the middle of the night. I felt my heart beating in my ears."

"Do you think you should be going on this trip today? It's not too late to pull out."

"Oh yes, dear. I wouldn't miss it for the world."

"Ok …" Mum Matthews was very uncertain. "But you must ring me if you get worse – right?"

"Yes, don't worry. Now come on. We'll be late!"

Mum managed to park easily and bought a ticket that gave her two hours. That would be enough to sit with her mother, have a coffee and make sure she got on her train properly. They settled down in the newly modernised station coffee house. Mum went to get the drinks and thought she'd treat her mother to a vanilla slice. She was sure to get plenty of napkins as her hands would get very sticky eating these. She paid and turned with her tray to where her mother was sitting and was instantly was alarmed to see two station officials talking in quite a serious manner to her mother. Other customers were getting up from their untouched tea and coffee and were moving away.

Mum Matthews dropped her tray on empty table and sprinted to her mum. "Mum, what's wrong?"

"Is this your mother?" This was a man named Jim, according to his name badge. Next to him was another station official who name badge read Paul. "I think we should move her to that space over there. She's struggling to breathe. I think she might be having a heart attack. My mum had one last year and looked just like this."

"Yes … yes … it's my mother." Mum Matthews was stunned. She felt weak. Useless. All over the place.

"Ok. Please can you ring 999 and tell them it's your mum and she's having a suspected heart attack. Tell me when you've made the call and let them know where we are. And don't worry, we've been fully trained in first aid."

Mum nodded and turned to go make the call.

Jim called quickly after her, "Oh! What's your mum's name?"

"It's Mary."

Mum Matthews left, her phone to her ear, and Jim turned back to Mary. "Ok. Don't worry, Mary … we're going to move you over to the wall here, so you have some more room." They moved Mary to the position. "Sit down on the floor with your back against the wall and your knees up. We'll just loosen this blouse to help you breathe better."

"Does she have any allergies?" Jim asked Mum.

"No."

"Paul, go and get the aspirin. Ok, Mary … we're going to get you to chew one. It will help."

Mary looked grey and she was covered in sweat. She was drifting in and out. Closing her eyes.

"Now stay with us, Mary. Where are you off to today, love?"

"To see my sister…" Her eyes closed.

"Stay awake for me, Mary. Are you on any medication?"

She opened her eyes. "Yes but it would take too long to name them all. Ha!"

"Is that right, Mary." Jim smiled.

At that point, Paul arrived back with the Aspirin and Jim turned away from Mary for a moment, reaching out his hand for the pain medication.

"Jim, careful!" Paul cried.

Jim looked back. Mary had slipped so that she lay on her back on the floor. Jim gripped her shoulders tight and shook. "Come on, Mary, speak to me, love. Where does your sister live?" Nothing. Jim opened her airway by putting two fingers under her chin and placing his other two fingers on her forehead and pulling her head back. He then got down and looked down her chest to see if she was breathing.

Mum Matthews came back at this point. "The ambulance is on its … Mum!?"

"Please, phone them back now and say she is not breathing. They will be here a lot quicker."

Mum Matthews was terrified and frozen to the spot staring at her mum who now had tinges of blue around her mouth.

"*Do it now!*" Jim shouted, jolting her out of her trance and she quickly called 999 again. "Paul, go and get our defib."

Jim started CPR (Cardiopulmonary Resuscitation). He undid Mary's coat and got it to the side. He interlocked his fingers and placed the heel of his hand in the centre of her chest, in line with her nose. He then started pumping down on Mary's chest. He counted out 30 chest compressions. He then moved himself to the top of Mary's head, opened her airway by tilting her head back and gave two breaths. He put a gap in-between the breaths so that he could see her chest rise and fall. It did. He moved back to the chest and counted out a further 30 chest compressions.

Mum Matthews asked in a quiet voice, "Is she coming back round?"

"No, she won't come back until we've used the defibrillator." Jim replied, just as Paul came back with their defib and started getting it out of its case.

Mum Matthews jumped into action then. "I can breathe into my mother while you do that?"

"Yeah, that would be good." Jim gave her a big smile.

Paul got his scissors out and cut off Mary's blouse and bra and wiped the adrenaline sweat off her torso. Jim and Mum Matthews worked as a team. Jim gave 30 chest compressions followed by her 2 breaths. Paul fitted the electrodes from the defib and turned the machine on.

"Do not touch the casualty, analysing heart rhythm," The machine commanded them. Everyone stood back.

The machine repeated its command. A shock was advised. They could hear the sirens of the ambulance. It was comforting, like the cavalry coming over the hill. "Push the orange shock button now." Another command. Mary's body twitched and jumped slightly when the shock was given. There were no signs of life. If it had worked they should have seen her normal colour return, her eyes opening, her Carotid arteries moving in her kneck and her chest rising and falling. They kept working on her. 30 compressions, 2 breaths, 30 compressions, 2 breaths. It was going to be 2 minutes until the next shock.

When the paramedics arrived they told them to carry on. They were doing well. One gave Mary an injection of adrenaline. This would quicken her heart rate and widen her airway and arteries. The other paramedic put a bag mask on Mary and connected it to an oxygen cylinder. They still had to keep her head back to get oxygen into her lungs but loads was getting in now.

"Do not touch the casualty, analysing heart rhythm," The machine sang out again.

The next shock worked and Mary came round. She was very disoriented as they loaded her into the back of the ambulance.

The paramedics praised everyone at the scene their excellent work. "You have really given Mary a fighting chance," he said.

Mum Matthews went with the paramedics and her mum to hospital and left her there a few hours later looking much better even though her chest really hurt.

Activity:

1. **RESEARCH: DEFIBRILLATOR**

A. What does a defibrillator do? Why are defibrillators an important piece of equipment to save lives?

B Draw a picture of a defibrillator. Label all the different parts and try to explain what they do.

CPR stands for CARDIO, PULMONARY and RESUSCITATION. Try to explain what each word means:

Cardio =

Pulmonary =

Resuscitation =

Draw a diagram of Jim giving Mary CPR

Include:

Where you kneel to perform CPR

Where you place your hands

How many chest compressions you perform

How many rescue breaths are given

Drowning and Bleeding

The summer holidays were finally here and the Matthews family were going to spend two weeks camping in France like they did every year. They all loved it.

The day before they left, they all spent some time making sure everything was ready for the trip. Dad Matthews was making sure the mechanics of the trailer worked properly, especially the brakes. The gas bottle was still full enough from last year. Mum Matthews was getting all the cutlery, plates and pans out to make sure they were serviceable and were clean. The water pump always needed mending and she was a genius at this. Jake and Lola were making sure that their packing was sorted and that they had enough to do in the back of the car.

All set. They were heading to the Ardeche this year. A two week cultural tour that would involve a lot of kayaking. It was going to be action packed and exciting. There were some stretches of that river that were quite challenging. Some rapids and weirs needed attention and care. It could be treacherous.

Barely five minutes after setting off, Dad Matthews realised that the car needed fuel! Coming back from paying, he popped his head in the back, all smiles. "Are you kids OK? You look snug back there." The car was already beginning to get that lived in 'hum' of sweaty armpits.

Lola groaned. "Are we there yet?"

Dad Matthews just raised his eyes to the sky and got on with the driving. It was going to be a long journey.

Many, *many* miles and hours and rest stop loo breaks later, they were in France and had found their campsite. It didn't take too long to get their basecamp read and it looked good. The awning had even gone up without a fight. Mum Matthews had silk flowers arranged in a hanging basket. It was home from home. The campsite was well chosen. It had tennis courts, a huge swimming pool with diving boards and a bar/restaurant. The live entertainment saw some top quality bands and crooners. The stream that ran through the site and the trees that canopied the camping areas gave it a feeling of freshness, tranquillity and beauty. The hills of the Massif Centrale could be clearly seen in the background to the East.

The next day, the first full day of their holiday, they were taken to the river in the minibus at the campsite. They were all going to kayak down the River Ardeche. They would do this in sections starting today at the top. Each time they would be dropped off with all their gear and picked up at the end. It was exciting. It was also going to be very difficult.

The driver of the minibus had no concept of speed or which side of the road he should be on. On entering one village on the way through to the river he saw a friend sitting outside a restaurant having a brandy (even though it was 9 a.m.!) and he just drove up to the place so that he could shake hands without getting fully out of his bus. He then sped off knocking tables and chairs out of the way. The kayaks he carried on the roof still had water sloshing around inside them and this was cascading down the windscreen which was already a bug graveyard. His speed increased despite having no visibility whatsoever. Dad Matthews decided that whatever the river offered it would not be as challenging as this journey.

They were all issued with a kayak, life jackets, paddles and a map of the river with the rendezvous clearly marked. The guide issued a warning about how to approach certain rapids. He also advised that this was a dam released white water route so there will be guaranteed fast flowing, exciting water – though that did, of course, make it more dangerous.

Dad Matthews was not keen on that news and was issuing his own safety chat to his brood. They were not to get separated. If one got too far ahead, they were to find still water and wait for the others. If one capsized, they must eject themselves by straightening their legs and pushing up and out through the canopy. The kayak will right itself and they would have to swim and grab it later.

"Let's enjoy it," Dad said, "but let's be safe." Off they went.

At first, the river was benign. They and what seemed like hundreds of others were gently paddling through still, deep water. The light glinting off the leaves of overhanging branches dappled on the river. It was idyllic.

The first signs of action were soon ahead: they could see the angle of the river change against the massive wall of rock plunging downwards. The noise changed, they could now hear the roar of the rapids in the distance. The Matthews all lined up for the final preparations.

Dad was animated. "Right, let's go for it. Even though you think you don't want to you must point your kayak into the fastest flowing water. You will then avoid the rocks. If you hit rocks they will spin you all around. Just get yourself facing down river … keep looking for the wall and follow the flow of water downwards. They don't last long these rapids and we'll soon be downstream in calm water. Enjoy it. Everyone OK?"

"Yes!" came the quick response.

"Lola, you come with me. Jake, stay close to Mum. Let's go." He sounded like a marine commando leading his amphibious landing party.

The first few sections were easily tackled and provided good practice. Some people were getting in a right tangle and some parties had escaped to a pool under some trees. They looked scared. The river plunged down at some height and speed in the next race and the extra water in the river made it move very fast. It was exhilarating. The Matthews family were doing well. Good technique. No boulders hit and they were all picking good lines on their descent. This section was steep, tough and long. It took all their wits and concentration.

Suddenly, they were in a section with no clear route and boulders seemed to lie everywhere. A guy had got his kayak lodged in between two boulders and he had capsized. It was like an arrow hitting its target. The kayak was quivering within the boulders. His friends were alarmed and gesticulating, shouting and screaming for help. The trouble was that his friends and loved ones were being taken rapidly downstream and there was no way to get back upstream unless you were a salmon! The guy in the kayak was now nowhere to be seen.

Dad Matthews acted swiftly. He wedged his kayak alongside and jumped onto the two boulders. He balanced as water surged all around him. Mum had the back end of the Frenchman's kayak and on 1 … 2 … 3 they flipped it over and up he came. He was not in a good shape. He had blood pouring from his head and he looked delirious.

"Let's get him into this pool." Dad had noticed a pool in an oasis of chaos to the left of the boulders. They heaved him into it. "You two, wedge yourself in those rocks so you don't fly off!" he shouted to Lola and Jake who looked bewildered and apprehensive.

Dad got the guy to speak to him but he was slumping all the time. "Phone 112 and tell them what's happened. Say, he's unconscious with head lacerations and he has been drowning. Tell me what they say, love." Mum Matthews went to her waterproof tub on her kayak, took out her phone and called the number.

Dad Matthews dragged the guy out onto the hardened mud bank. He rested his back against a rock and bent both his legs so his knees were up because if he was left lying down with his legs up, it would be too much blood rushing to his already damaged head. He wanted the blood from his legs to come to his brain but the blood from his thighs was going to be enough. In the absence of a first aid kit, Dad Matthews got the sleeve of his thin fleece and wrapped it tightly around the guy's head wound. It soon absorbed the blood and seemed to be helping stem the bleeding.

Dad realised the man had stopped breathing so he started performing 5 mouth-to-mouth 'rescue' breaths on the man in an effort to bring him back – it worked. The man rolled over and vomited into the river. At least he was awake. Dad kept chatting to the man. He was reassuring him and keeping him alert.

"There's nothing happening, just no reception!" Mum Matthews cried, hanging up the phone. Their location was just too remote to get reception.

"OK love," Dad Matthews shouted above the roar of the rapids, "he seems to be coming round but we still need to get him to a hospital. We can't risk secondary drowning."

Secondary drowning was very serious, and Mum Matthews knew that. It's where a person may have been resuscitated but not taken to a hospital to dry their lungs out. It can cause the person to die later on.

"I know, we need to get him to a hospital but what can we do? I can't get through to them."

"You can text 112 for emergency services! Don't you remember?"

Dad Matthews had registered all their phones for this very important and useful service by texting REGISTER to 112. It was very simple and one day it could save a life – like today!

"Yeah, I remember. I'll try that now." Mum Matthew's thumbs were going like the clappers. Nothing seemed to be happening for ages. There must be a weak signal because of the deep river valley. After what seemed like an age, Mum Matthews shouted, "Hey, they've replied. They are on their way."

Activity:

In the table below, the dangers of this trip are listed. Say why they ARE dangers and design a sign that will warn others and reflect that danger to other people. One sign is to be designed for each danger. Make them a triangular shape.

What is the danger?	Why is it a danger?	Warning Sign
No fuel in the car		
Swimming Pool on campsite		
Dangerous driving by the mini-bus driver		
Kayaking down the river		

The final Activity

Make a leaflet!

Your leaflet should be an A4 piece of paper folded in an attractive way and written and drawn/coloured on both sides. This will be an information giving leaflet that teaches other children about different conditions and how to treat them. **Pick ANY topic that you have studied in this book.**

The leaflet should clearly explain how we know that people are suffering (what the signs and symptoms are) and what we should do about it (what treatment can we give?). It should be informative but as clear and interesting as possible. Turn on the style! It should have lots of diagrams and pictures as well as writing.

A note from the author

Hello everyone,

I hope that you have enjoyed *Greenbank Primary: First Aid Brought to Life*.

The intention was education and I hope you have learned a lot. All I can encourage you to do is to keep learning. It's so important. I hope that you do keep learning the real techniques. The joy of being able to save somebody's life is incalculable, both to you as the life-saver but crucially to the survivor and their family.

Good luck and be kind.

Malcolm Sweetlove

Acknowledgements

Professor Lawrence Cotter, Dr John Miller, Dr Tony Moriarty, Dr Clare Rayner, Sue Warhurst, Aston Kelly (my on-stage son) and Hugh MacDonald (University of Manchester Medical School).

Sir Alex Ferguson CBE, Lizzie Jones MBE, Glenn Hoddle and Katie Zelem for their encouragement and support.

Maggie Kneen. Fabulous illustrator; an artistic genius.

Natalie and Chris Parsons for their technical advice and support. Catherine Sweetlove for her advice, patience and proof reading.

Byron and Alex McGuinness for their reading and advice alongside Pharmacist Farhan Ali and his children Yusuf, Ibrahim and Ismail Ali.

Libby, Rhianna and Dylan Ashton. Alison, Chris, Lucy, Emily and Thomas Linton. Adam and Robert Foy.

Helmshore Primary School: Christine Myers (Headteacher), Nicola Haworth, Lindsay Kelly (Year 6 teachers whose advice and suggestions are key to this book), Lucia and Molly Kelly who have all given me so much help. Especially the Year 6 classes at Helmshore who, during the Covid-19 virus in 2020, worked through the book and gave such helpful and positive feedback. To Christine Gregory who is such a dedicated member of staff with a totally positive attitude despite suffering MND.

Kirsty White. Ann and Dave Elmer. John, Anne and Rachel Strivens for their support and Jonathan Strivens, senior paramedic, for all his excellent advice and help over the years.

Alan and Sharon Sweetlove for all their support.

Rachel Basdeo for her invaluable advice.

Bury Hospice, Springhill Hospice, Rossendale Hospice, Royal Oldham Hospital, Tower Minden Family Health Care and Bury NHS CCG for whom I train and who have helped me over the years.

Alan Cunningham for being an inspirational survivor of cardiac arrest and a dear friend and Lucie Collinge who saved his life working together with me on 28 August 2019.

Inspired by Worksafe Training Systems.

BV - #0032 - 180621 - C16 - 210/210/7 - PB - 9781912964772 - Gloss Lamination